A Bannock Boy Christmas

Welcome

A Bannock Boy Christmas

A Bannock Boy Christmas

Bannock Boy was getting super excited, his second favorite holiday was almost here. His first favorite holiday was of course Halloween, the time he could be anything he wanted to be.

Did you guess it? It is Christmas of course. It was now November 1 and there was a chill in the air as he raked up leaves in his yard. His mother had chores for him to complete in order to get his weekly allowance.

The crisp November air gave his cheeks a real rosy glow to him, it also made his think of food and bright red apples. He was getting tired though as there was a lot of leaves to clean up and he had to take down all his Halloween decorations.

This had to all be done before he could begin to decorate for Christmas. There was still no snow on the ground, so he was okay. He was tired and wanted to take a rest under a huge oak tree that was nearby. He was working hard and thought he deserved a rest, so he put his rake down and pushed some of the leaves into a pile and made a pillow for himself. Just a short rest as he closed his eyes with dreams of Christmas and all the gifts he would receive.

He had been asleep for mere minutes it seemed and he was awoken by a noise, he thought it might be a skunk, he certainly did not want to get sprayed and try to explain to this mother that he had fallen asleep on the job. He rubbed his eyes in attempt to wake up and get his bearing about himself. As his vision cleared, he saw an incredibly old man with a cane and white hair and a huge white beard. He did not recall an old man like that in the neighborhood and he knew his mother did not want him to speak to strangers. But there was something about the old man that made him feel at ease. He did not know what it was, but he felt okay and safe. The old man spoke to Bannock Boy, "Good morning my boy, how are you doing?" Bannock Boy answered the old man, "I am okay, just tired and excited for Christmas, trying to get our yard cleaned up."

Bannock Boy lived alone with his mother, his father had died, and his mother worked two jobs to support them, so his mother relied on him a lot. He had to grow up fast and try to fill some big shoes. But sometimes Bannock Boy resented all the work his

A Bannock Boy Christmas

mother asked him to do. Sometimes, he just wanted to play and have fun, this work really sucked. It made him angry a lot, he wished his father were still here, he really missed him. Sometimes, and he knew it was not right, but he was angry at God for taking his father away. He was jealous as all his friends still had their father and they did fun things for their dad.

The old man proceeded to ask Bannock Boy what he liked most about Christmas. A huge grin came on Bannock Boy's face and he was so excited he could stop himself from stuttering. Before Bannock Boy answered he thought, I do not even know the old man's name. If he knew his name, then he would not be a stranger.

So, he asked the old man for his name. The old man answered, "My boy you can call me Nick". That made Bannock Boy happy as now he was not speaking with a stranger. Bannock Boy proceeded to tell Nick that the best thing about Christmas to him was gifts, gifts, and more gifts. The smile from the old man's face began to dim and fade away. There even seemed to be a tear form in his eye.

Bannock Boy really did not understand the reaction of the old man, he thought, was not gifts the most important part of Christmas?

The old man made a gesture to Bannock Boy to sit back down in the bed of leaves. "Boy I want to tell you a story and some Metis History".

A Bannock Boy Christmas

The Métis people have long placed a great emphasis on maintaining strong relationships among families, extended families, and communities, particularly when work was hard and the future uncertain. Nowhere were these bonds of kinship and friendship better renewed than during Christmas and New Year's celebrations.

While Christmas Day was largely a religious event for most Métis communities in the late nineteenth and early twentieth centuries, it remained festive. Many Métis Elders have recounted that families spent Christmas Eve by attending Midnight Mass, occasionally singing hymns in Cree or French, and then having a large supper and party known as Réveillon.

However, most celebrating during the holiday season was reserved for New Year's Day. Early on the morning of Christmas Day, families traveled by horse and sleigh to loved ones' homes and stayed until late in the evening. Prior to this gathering, mothers and daughters prepared food for days to ensure everyone would be well fed.

Christmas and New Years' fare included beignes (fried bannock), boulettes (meat balls), rababou (stew), chokecherries or saskatoon berries served with cream and sugar, puddings, pemmican, wild game, as well as tea, unlike the commercialism, which permeates our holiday season, traditional Métis Christmas celebrations were modest.

A Bannock Boy Christmas

Children were an integral part of New Year's celebrations. On New Year's Eve, children received presents from their parents, generally small gifts of food.

After receiving their presents, on the morning of New Year's Day, children thanked and blessed their parents, and families hugged and kissed one another.

Wow, that was a lot of information for Bannock Boy to take in, sure did not mention a lot of gifts. It did mention a lot of food though and the mention of food made Bannock Boy very hungry. The old man asked Bannock Boy, "What is your favorite Christmas food?" Bannock Boy of course loved Bannock but he drifted to the Christmas treat Kokum would make. It had to be "pudding in a bag". The old man smiled and said, "That is my favorite too, do you know how it is made?" Bannock Boy shook his head. "Let me explain," said the old man.

"Potato sac" or "pudding in a bag" was a favorite Métis dessert served at Christmas dinners and included dried fruit such as raisins or currents. The sweet dessert had the texture of fruit cake and was eaten warm with a brown sugar sauce poured over it. This was made from brown sugar and butter and heated on the stove. Bread pudding was another cherished recipe made with brown sugar. Wow, Bannock Boy was getting so very hungry. The old man went on. "Tourtierre" was another common specialty savory pie served during holiday meal gatherings; however, the ingredients for what makes this pie traditional were controversial. Some argued that traditional tourtierre should only be made purely with pork, and never to include beef, whereas others stated that a combination of beef and pork ingredients still constituted a traditional pie.

The old man went on to say, "We would dance the old-time dances and the RED RIVER Jig, reel of four, reel of eight, double jig, strip the willow, rabbit chase, Tucker circle, drops of brandy, and all the half-breed dances.

There were always lots of fiddlers. Nearly every man could play the fiddle. Then we would go to another family. I tell you; we had a regular good time. We had lots to eat and drink …. This feasting lasted about ten days." A brief tear escaped from the old man's face and he said, " I have rambled enough and kept you from your work, thank you for talking to me young man, I so long for the good old days, I miss my family and our times spent going to Church and being together."

Bannock Boy said goodbye to the old man and started to finish up raking the leaves. After he finished, he was to go to Kokum's house to eat and he was super hungry from all his work. With his raking done he decided to make his way to Kokum's house as his mother was still at work, boy did he ever work up an appetite.

A Bannock Boy Christmas

Bannock Boy arrived at Kokum's house out of breath and hungry like a bear. As he entered the door, Kokum gave Bannock Boy a huge kiss and told him supper was almost done. She asked Bannock Boy how his day was. Bannock Boy told Kokum about the old man Nick he had met as he was raking leaves and all the stories, he told him. But again, nothing too much about gifts. Kokum smiled and said to Bannock Boy, do you think Christmas is just about gifts?" Bannock Boy thought it was and ya right good food too.

Kokum said to Bannock Boy, "Let me tell you a few of my Christmas memories as we wait for supper to get done." Bannock Boy nodded and sat at the table. Kokum began, "Christmas is a time for traditions and being with family. It is a special time when we express our culture and our love of family. I can remember a Christmas from 1936, at Turtle Mountain. The old French and Indian spirit of Christmas begins at Christmas Eve with midnight mass. After the services are over, we all begin to greet our friends. Then we hurry to get home to the little ones and do our part with Santa Clause.

We are awakened in the morning very early, by the sounds of little bugles, trumpets, drums and all sorts of merrymaking toys. The little children with their mouths filled with candy and laughter make all happy and we wish the world a Merry Christmas!

When supper was over, individual jigging began. This is a special feature of our dances.

A Bannock Boy Christmas

The fiddler, with the fiddle casually against his ribs, struck up the Red River jig. One of the best jiggers chose his partner and began... We also played a lot of games at Christmas time. We loved the Map Game. One of two teams hid while the captain drew a map for the opposing team, detailing the position of the hidden children. The map could be made very confusing but had to be legible. The opposing team would have to find the hidden children using this map. Once all the children were found, the opposing team hid, and the captain drew a map. At each turn, the captain changed to allow every child an opportunity to draw a map.

We Métis also enjoyed playing cards – an activity very popular among our voyageur ancestors. In fact, in the times of York boat transportation, men frequently played poker to pass the time when weather would not permit them to travel. Many Métis, except those who do not participate because of religious principles, enjoy card games. Card games can spring up wherever and whenever time and space permits. I remember, women cooking for social events could quickly get a game going while the food is in the oven.

I also remember A favorite children's card game in St. Laurent, Manitoba, was called "La Penitence." Losers of the game would be given a penance to complete. Examples of penance include walking around the house in the dark holding the ace of spades, which represented to some people the fork of the devil or planting a kiss on a visitor's baldhead!"

Kokum said, "Did you know New Year's Day was usually held at the grandparents' home and was a special time for families, as cousins, aunts, and uncles attended. It was an occasion for the eating of all sorts of food with people traveling from house to house, dining, dancing, and visiting. While visiting house-to-house, everybody would shake hands and kiss, a carry-over of French-Canadian tradition. As a result, some Métis called New Year's Day "Ochetookeskaw" or kissing day." Kokum told Bannock Boy her favorite food at Christmas time was moose. Kokum asked Bannock Boy, have you ever heard of the moose story?" Bannock Boy shook his head.

Kokum began, "How the people hunted the moose. A family of moose was sitting in the lodge when a pipe came floating in through the door, passing close to each of the Moose People until it reached the youngest of the young bull moose. He took the pipe and started to smoke it. The old moose knew that it was a pipe the human beings were smoking to ask for success in their hunt. Now, tomorrow, they will find us, he said. But the young moose was not afraid, for he thought he could outrun them.

When the Moose People reached the edge of the forest the next day, they caught the scent of the hunters. The thin crust on the snow made it hard for the moose to move quickly. The young moose was still sure he could outrun the hunters, but the hunters were wearing snowshoes. They followed him until he tired, and then they killed him. They thanked him for giving himself to them so they could survive. They treated his body with care, soothing his spirit.

When the young moose woke up in his bed that night, he said to the others, "Those hunters treated me with respect. It is right for us to allow the human beings to catch us." And so, it is to this day. Those hunters who show respect for the moose are always the ones who are successful when they hunt."

Bannock Boy had a sense of wonder in his eyes, he loved his Kokum's stories, he learned so much about being Metis.

Kokum went on to say, "A traditional teaching amongst the First Nations of Turtle Island, is that before the Europeans crossed the ocean, native elders had visions of people coming from the east with messages from the Creator." Kokum said to Bannock Boy, "this is also a story my Kokum told me. The Handsome Fellow Legend refers to a Creek leader named Chief Hobbythacco, which translates in English as "handsome fellow". According to tradition, chiefs were given gifts throughout the year, especially during summer months, and the chiefs would then share their bounty with tribal members. Some Native Americans encourage children to believe The Handsome Fellow is responsible for leaving presents on Christmas Day while others believe Santa comes to visit. Bannock Boy did you know when I was a small girl our Christmas celebrations include a manger scene and a recreation of the three Wise Men offering gifts to the Christ child? Some Indians observe a similarity between the Chiefs of the Great Nations and the Wise Men, as well as the act of bestowing newborn babe with gifts to that of the Great Thunderbird telling the braves in fields about the birth." Bannock Boy's head was spinning, how he loved the stories that Kokum told him. He cherished any time he got to spend with her.

Now it was time to eat, and Bannock Boy loved to eat, and he knew Kokum had some hot bannock for him to enjoy. As they both sat at the kitchen table enjoying Kokum's moose roast, they both smiled at each other and laughed.

"And so, to this very day, those Metis who honor and show respect for the moose will always be successful in their hunts and rewarded with meat when they need it." said Kokum.

Bannock Boy was sad about the young moose being shot and killed by the Metis men. Kokum said to him, "One day Bannock Boy when you are older, you will understand this."

It was still light out so it was safe for Bannock Boy to walk the short distance home as his mother would be home from work by now. He gave Kokum a huge kiss and hug and thanked her for the great stories and the wonderful food. He was stuffed.

A Bannock Boy Christmas

Bannock Boy rushed through the door and said hello to his mother, who he knew was going to be tired. He had a surprise for her. Kokum had made a special plate of food for her. His mother said, "Hello Bannock Boy, how was your day?" Bannock Boy was talking a mile a minute and said he had a wonderful supper at Kokum's house, and she told some of her super stories, he loved that. "Mom," said Bannock Boy, "Kokum made a plate of food for you, her special moose roast." Mom had a huge smile on her face, she was tired as she had to work a double shift at work and the thought of making something to eat was the last thing on her mind.

"Bannock Boy, thank you, you have no idea how much that means to me." Bannock Boy decided to do his homework at the kitchen table while his mother ate her supper. Bannock Boy knew that no matter how tired his mother was, she always made time to tuck him into bed and tell him a story to help him drift off to sleep. He wondered what the story would be tonight, he loved stories.

His mother was washing up and getter herself ready for bed as well. She was worried though, money would be very tight this year, being a single mother and she knew Bannock Boy had a huge list of presents he wanted to have Santa bring him this year. A tear began to drift down her cheek, she felt helpless and just did not know how she would be able to do it. Maybe if she tried to tell Bannock Boy the true meaning of Christmas by the way of bedtime stories, he would not be as disappointed, it was worth a try.

Bannock Boy was already in his bed when his mother came to tuck him in and begin the night's story. Mother said, "Tonight Bannock Boy I will tell you the story of two Christmas Angels." Bannock Boy started to get excited, a Christmas story. Mother began, "This story my boy is about two angel friends. One of the two angels wore pink robes and the other wore blue robes. These angels were known for singing lovely duets and praised the glory of God. They also played trumpets made from pure silver that were believed to be the most melodious sounds ever heard by man.

The angels, who were popular for their musical talents, led and conducted the orchestra for many angels, several times. One day, their orchestra lead, shared wonderful news to the members of the angelic orchestra. He said that God decided to send his 'Son' to live among "HIS" people. On hearing this news, the angels were overjoyed. The cherubs decided to prepare a musical event for the most important occasion in history. The musical event was expected to be flawless and only angels with the best voices were chosen to sing. The orchestra leader questioned his orchestra whether they knew what to do and for what purpose they sang. The angel, dressed in pink, answered by saying that the "LORD" wanted the angels to show themselves to the shepherds, who lived in the hills of Bethlehem, and also added that the shepherds might be afraid because would have never witnessed angels in their lives. The angel in blue, added to what the pink angel had to say, by saying that the angels could remove the fear of the shepherds by singing and declaring the arrival of the 'savior' on human lands. On hearing the answers of both the angels, the orchestra leader smiled and nodded.

On the day of Jesus Christ's birth, the Christmas angels set out to meet the shepherds. Several angels appeared in front of the shepherds and played few notes to rejoice the birth of baby Jesus. The shepherds were awestruck. Never were they confronted by divine beings in their life. This was a first. The shepherds were amazed with this sudden appearance and their hearts were filled with humility and love for God. The angels sang praises for God and spread happiness all around. With their angelic voices they spoke the words - "Glory to God in the highest, and on earth peace, good will to men".

"Bannock Boy," said mother, "Did you know angels are regarded as messengers of God and are believed to serve as an intermediary between 'Man' and God? The wings of angels signify innocence and purity. Angels are regarded as divine, immortal beings that spread happiness and peace. Today, during the "Nativity scenes", Christmas angels are depicted as singing and playing musical instruments to the shepherds. Christmas angels are hung on Christmas trees for a more divine ambience." Bannock Boy, loved angels and loved the story and said to his

A Bannock Boy Christmas

mother, "One more story, please mother, please."
Even though his mother was very tired from work,
she thought the more stories about the true meaning
of Christmas the better to soften the blow about not
being to afford gifts for Christmas. Mother said,
"Okay my boy, just one more story and off to bed."
Bannock Boy smiled and said, "thanks mom, I will go
to sleep after this last story, I promise."

"Bannock Boy, do you know the legend of the
Christmas Star?" Bannock Boy shook his head. "Well
my boy here it goes. A new star was seen in the sky,
along with other stars, one fine night and this star
was so radiant that its bright rays spread light as
bright as day on the gray hills of Bethlehem. The
shepherds, who were resting after a hectic day, saw
this strange, bright star and were frightened because
of the unusual shine. Immediately, to their surprise,
an angel came to them and said: "Do not be afraid; the
star has come to bring you good tidings of great joy,
and to show you the place where a little baby is born,
a little babe whose name is Jesus, and who will give
peace and joy to the whole world." The angel
disappeared after saying this and the shepherds
decided to go and see the child. They left their flock of
sheep resting on the hillside and took their crook.

The shepherds started towards Bethlehem, following
the bright star and reached the stable where Jesus
Christ was born. They bowed the baby who was
cradled in a manger. It was the same star that
appeared before the three wise men who noticed the

star moving. They understood that it was some omen and began to follow it. These wise men too, reached Bethlehem and bowed down before the baby and presented him with the various gifts that they had got with them. The star, which casted the bright light and led the shepherds and wise men to Bethlehem, then went back to heaven. The Christmas star is not just a colorful decor; it signifies peace and high hopes. It gives you the ray of hope that the Son of God will help you confront and conquer every difficult situation you come across. It shows that every good thing comes from within and that there is a silver lining in every dark cloud."

Mother looked over and Bannock Boy was asleep with a smile on his face. Time for mother herself to head to bed, she was tired and had another hard day of work ahead of her.

Christmas time was drawing near, and Bannock Boy was excited and wondered when they would get their Christmas tree. The one they had before burned up in a fire and he was worried they would not have a tree. Before his mother headed to work and he was to go to school, Bannock Boy asked his mother, "mother when can we get our Christmas tree? We are making decorations at school and I have no where to hang them up." Mother looked at Bannock Boy with a weary face and said, 'Bannock Boy go to Kokum's house after school and then we can discuss the Christmas tree." Bannock Boy said okay and left for school.

A Bannock Boy Christmas

After school he headed to Kokum's house and she was ready for him with a warm piece of bannock and a warm smile. "Kokum, I cannot wait until we can get our Christmas tree, I have made a lot of Christmas decorations at school." "Well my boy, I am sure your mother has this all figured out and you will get one soon. But for now, what does a Christmas tree mean to you?" Well Bannock Boy said, "It is a place to put all my presents under and put my school decorations on." Kokum smiled and said, "Bannock Boy how about a story and another piece of bannock?" "Yeah", said Bannock Boy.

"Well my boy, here goes. Christmas tree, perhaps, has its origin in the Vikings from North Europe, who took evergreen trees as an inspiration to struggle on with life, during winters and as a reminder that spring season will soon come again. Many Pagan festivals used Christmas trees and later, they were imbibed into Christian festivals too. The custom of decorating Christmas trees during the festival of Christmas came from England and France during the ancient times, when Druids used to decorate oak trees with candles and fruits at the time of their harvest festivals. Ancient Romans too are known to decorate trees during Saturnalia - their harvest festival - with trinkets. German Christians were the first to incorporate Christmas trees in their homes. At places, where trees were not so readily available, they used wooden pyramids as artificial Christmas trees. The first known Christmas tree that came into limelight

A Bannock Boy Christmas

was the one decorated by Prince Albert of English Royalty, who decorated his tree with candies and gingerbread along with candles and fruits. German immigrants brought the custom from Europe to America and by 1800s, it had become a household craze. Ancient Christmas tree ornaments included cookies, popcorn, apples, and nuts. Today, Christmas tree holds a special significance of Christmas and is an inevitable part of the festival."

Kokum said to Bannock Boy, "You might find these interesting to you:

Interesting & Fun Facts About Christmas

The Christian church fixed 25 December in 440 A.D. as the day for the celebration of Christmas.

The word 'Christmas' is an old English word and is a contracted version of 'Christ's Mass'.

The word 'X-Mas' is derived from Greek, because in Greek, 'X' symbolizes Christ.

The tradition of ringing church bells on Christmas morning dates to the medieval times. The ringing bells symbolize the birth of Jesus Christ.

The tradition of gift-giving during Christmas has originated from the legendary characters of the Three Wise Men, who brought presents to Jesus, when he was born.

Many people believe that the legendary character Santa Claus is based on a real person named St.

A Bannock Boy Christmas

Nicholas. It is also believed that St. Nicholas brings in Christmas gifts, on the Eve of the festival.

According to the legends, St. Nicholas lived in 4th century AD. The Christian leader was very shy. He wanted to help the poor and the needy, therefore the decided to give money to them in secrecy.

Franklin Pierce was the first US President to decorate the White House with a beautifully adorned Christmas Tree.

The tradition of eating turkey on Christmas Day can be traced back to the Tudor Times and the reign of Henry VIII. He was the first man to eat turkey on the auspicious occasion.

While people generally greet each other by saying 'Merry Christmas', some priests in Australia prefer to believe that one should say 'Happy Christmas', because the word 'Merry' has connotations of 'getting drunk'.

Christmas cards were invented in 1843, a period of the Victorian Era.

Alabama was the first state to declare Christmas as an official holiday. It was recognized as a national holiday in America on June 26, 1870.

Poinsettia, the popular Christmas plant, reached the United States from Mexico in 1880s. The plant was named after Joel Poinsett.

A Bannock Boy Christmas

People began to make use of electric lights for their Christmas tree, in 1895.

Rudolph, the legendary reindeer of Santa Claus, was a creation of Montgomery Ward. He created it for the purpose of a holiday promotion, in the late 1930s.

The world's tallest Christmas tree was erected in America, in 1950. The tree was as high as 76 m.

Candy canes, one of the popular sweet treats used for Christmas, originally were straight white sticks of sugar candy. They were used as an embellishment for Christmas tree. The ends of the candy were bent by Cologne Cathedral, to symbolize shepherd's crook. The candy canes were given red stripes only in 20th century.

Although 'Jingle Bells' was first written for Thanksgiving, it gained immense popularity as a song associated with the celebration of Christmas.

Holly berries, the berries traditionally used for decorating Christmas mistletoe and wreath, are poisonous. On the other hand, poinsettia plants that are believed as poisonous are non-toxic.

Holy represents the crown worn by Lord Jesus Christ, when he was crucified, and the red color of the berries represents his blood.

Christmas is the season when the world witnesses the maximum sale of diamonds.

A Bannock Boy Christmas

Every year, during the Christmas season, more than a billion cards are sold in UK.

Christmas stockings were first hung in southern Europe.

In some parts of the world, banana trees are decorated at Christmas time, due to the unavailability of the original Christmas tree.

Original Christmas trees are grown predominantly in Alaska and Hawaii. All around the world, as much as 1,000,000 acres of land have been planted with Christmas trees.

Most artificial Christmas trees are manufactured in Hong Kong, Taiwan, and Korea."

Wow thought Bannock Boy that is a lot of interesting information.

Kokum had a secret that Bannock Boy knew nothing about. The same old man, Nick who Bannock Boy had met when he was raking leaves had stopped by and left a gift for Bannock Boy. It was a certificate for a free Christmas tree, it just had to be picked up. Kokum could hardly contain herself and decided to tell Bannock Boy about the mysterious visitor she had called, Nick. After supper Kokum asked Bannock Boy, "Do you know an old man named Nick?" At first Bannock Boy had to think a moment and then remembered that day when he had been raking leaves. I sure do Kokum. "Well he left an envelope for you the other day and he told me to make sure you got it."

Bannock Boy was so excited and opened it the moment Kokum gave it to him. Inside the envelope was a certificate for a free Christmas tree, there was also a note inside. It said, "From your friend Nick, enjoy your Christmas, you have learned so much about the real meaning of Christmas, Merry Christmas, Love Nick." Bannock Boy screamed with delight and was running around in Kokum's house. Bannock Boy forgot all about all the gifts he had hoped to receive, he was just thinking about all the decorations he had made at school and where he would place them on the Christmas tree, he was so excited.

Kokum said, "Bannock Boy, your mother is getting off early today from work to pick us both up to go get the Christmas tree." Yah, said Bannock Boy, I can hardly wait." So sure, enough mother was at Kokum's within half of an hour and they all dressed warm to go pick up the Christmas tree that Nick had gifted them. Once the tree was secured on the top of his mother's station wagon, they sang Christmas carols all the way home. Bannock Boy looked out of the car window and in the night sky he saw a star shining very brightly and it even looked like it blinked at him. He was very happy, but not about gifts, but about the gift of his family and the gift from the mysterious stranger named Nick.

A Bannock Boy Christmas

A Bannock Boy Christmas

Merry Christmas

A Bannock Boy Christmas

Fun Facts

Did you know......The oldest Christmas carol written in North America is believed to be 'Twas in the Moon of Wintertime. Jesuit missionary Jean de Brebeuf wrote the carol, somewhere around 1643, while at Sainte-Marie among the Hurons. In 1926, J. E. Middleton translated the hymn into English. Here it is:

'Twas in the moon of wintertime

When all the birds had fled

That mighty Gitchi Manitou

Sent angel choirs instead

Before their light the stars grew dim

And wond'ring hunters heard the hymn:

Jesus, your King, is born.

Jesus is born!

In excelsis gloria!

Within a lodge of broken bark,

The tender Babe was found

A ragged robe of rabbit skin

Enwrapped His beauty round

And as the hunter braves drew nigh,

The angel song rang loud and high:

A Bannock Boy Christmas

Jesus, your King, is born.

Jesus is born!

In excelsis gloria!

O children of the forest free,

O songs of Manitou

The Holy Child of earth and heav'n

Is born today for you

Come kneel before the radiant Boy

Who brings you beauty, peace, and joy:

Jesus, your King, is born.

Jesus is born!

In excelsis gloria!

Here is a great recipe for Christmas Bannock Cookies
that you can make with adult supervision.

Christmas Bannock Cookies

Makes 64 cookies.

1 1/2 cups flour

1/4 teaspoon salt

3/8 cup confectioners' sugar

1/3 cup finely minced candied fruit

A Bannock Boy Christmas

1/4 cup finely minced toasted almonds

3/4 cup unsalted butter, cut into pieces and slightly softened

1 1/2 tablespoons granulated sugar

Method

Preheat oven to 325 degrees. To prepare by hand: On a cool work surface, combine flour, salt, and sugar; stir to blend. Add fruit and almonds, tossing to coat fruit with flour mixture. Cut in butter with pastry blender or 2 knives until mixture resembles fine crumbs. To prepare in a food processor: In work bowl of food processor, combine flour, salt, and confectioners' sugar. Pulse briefly until just blended. Add fruit, almonds, and butter. Pulse several times until mixture resembles fine crumbs. Press dough into 8-inch-square baking pan; sprinkle with granulated sugar. Bake until lightly browned (about 30 minutes). Immediately cut into 1-inch squares. Leave in pan 10 minutes, then place cubes on wire rack to cool.

Here are some fun facts on the Red River Jig, this is a loved Metis Christmas tradition.

The Red River Jig or as it is known in Michif, "oayache mannin", the most famous Métis dance. It is considered an unofficial Métis anthem. The dance is a combination of Plains First Nations footwork with Scottish, Irish, and French-Canadian dance forms.

A Bannock Boy Christmas

There are three theories of the Red River Jig's origin. The first states that it was brought over from Lower Canada (now Québec) with the French-Canadian voyageurs and was originally called "La gigue du Bas Canada", or "La grande gigue simple". Métis fiddle player Fredrick Genthon said that he learned the jig from his father who had learned it in 1842 from a French Canadian named Lauterelle.

The second theory has its origins in the Red River Settlement. The theory states that the Scottish lived on one side of the river (either the Seine, Red or Assiniboine Rivers), and the French Canadians and Métis lived on the other. The Scots played bagpipes on the one side of the river, while the people on the other side listened. Then one night a man decided to imitate the bagpipes with his fiddle and played a sad tune, but then started playing a rollicking beat that made everyone want to dance. The final theory states that the tune originated at a Métis wedding in 1860 when Mr. Macdallas composed a new fiddle tune for the celebration, which Father Boucher, the wedding's officiating priest, dubbed the "Red River Jig".

The following is a sequence of the "Red River Jig" steps:

1. Back step four times.

2. Front step four times. Double.

3. Front step four times. Single.

4. Triple tap four times.

A Bannock Boy Christmas

5. Triple tap four times, accented right.

6. Triple tap four times, accented left.

7. Triple tap four times, accented right and left.

8. Triple tap four times, accented double.

9. Time tap.

10. Cross over handclasp with triple tap.

11. Right tap turn.

12. Triple tap four times.

13. Double tap four times.

14. Heel-toe step four times, right foot.

15. Heel-toe step four times, left foot.

16. Heel-toe step four times, double.

17. Triple tap, four times, half circle facing each other, cross over, handclasp to places.

Bannock Boy would like to wish you and your family a VERY MERRY CHRISTMAS and HAPPY NEW YEAR.

Merry Christmas in Cree - Mitho Makosi Kesikansi

Merry Christmas in Michif - Gayayr Nwel

A Bannock Boy Christmas

Extras

Silent Night Hymn

Silent night! Holy night!
All is calm, all is bright
Round yon virgin mother and child!
Holy infant, so tender and mild,
Sleep in heavenly peace!
Sleep in heavenly peace!

Silent night! Holy night!
Shepherds quake at the sight!
Glories stream from heaven afar,
Heavenly hosts sing Alleluia!
Christ the Saviour is born!
Christ the Saviour is born!

Silent night! Holy night!
Son of God, love's pure light
Radiant beams from thy holy face
With the dawn of redeeming grace,
Jesus, Lord, at thy birth!
Jesus, Lord, at thy birth!

A Bannock Boy Christmas

Coloring Pages

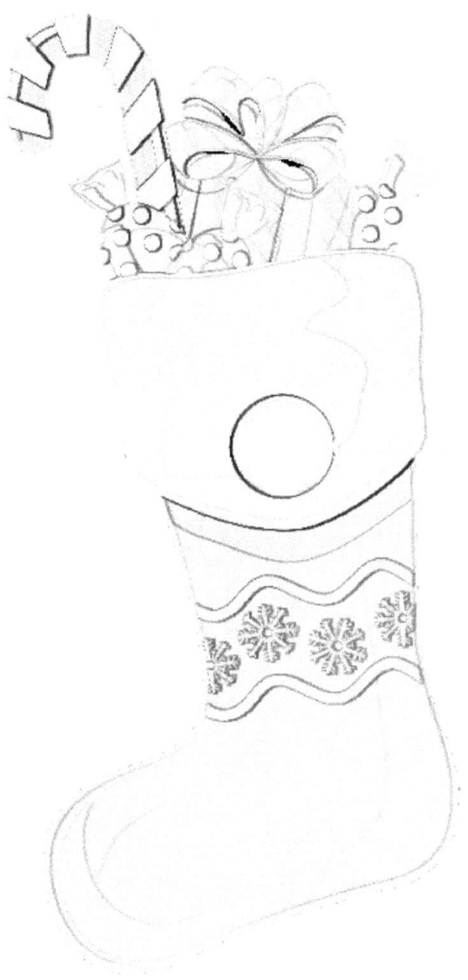

A Bannock Boy Christmas

A Bannock Boy Christmas

A Bannock Boy Christmas